G000097395

SHEARSMAN
135 & 136

SPRING 2023

EDITOR
TONY FRAZER

Shearsman magazine is published in the United Kingdom by
Shearsman Books Ltd
P.O. Box 4239
Swindon   SN3 9FL

Registered office: 30–31 St James Place, Mangotsfield, Bristol BS16 9JB
(this address not for correspondence)

www.shearsman.com

ISBN 978-1-84861-869-5
ISSN 0260-8049

Subscriptions and single copies

Current subscriptions – covering two double-issues, each 100–110 pages in length – cost £17 for delivery to UK addresses, £24 for the rest of Europe (including the Republic of Ireland), £28 for Asia & North America, and £30 for Australia, New Zealand and Singapore. Longer subscriptions may be had for a pro-rata higher payment. Purchasers in North America and Australia will find that buying single copies from online retailers there will be cheaper than subscribing, especially following the recent drastic price-rises for international mail. This is because copies are printed locally to meet such orders from online retailers. Following recent changes to the handling of cross-border transactions in the EU, purchasers in the EU (except for those in Ireland) are recommended to use EU-based online retailers, or the UK's The Book Depository, which can handle the new system.

Back issues from nº 63 onwards (uniform with this issue) cost £9.95 / $17 through retail outlets. Single copies can be ordered for £9.95 direct from the press, post-free within the UK, through the Shearsman Books online store, or from bookshops. Contact us regarding earlier issues (i.e. nos. 1–62), whether for single copies or a complete run.

Submissions

Shearsman operates a submissions-window system, whereby submissions may only be made during the months of March and September, when selections are made for the October and April issues, respectively. Submissions may be sent by mail or email, but email attachments are only accepted in PDF form. We aim to respond within 3 months of the window's closure, although we do sometimes take a little longer.

Acknowledgement

We are grateful to the Casanovas & Lynch Literary Agency, Barcelona, acting for the author's Estate, for permission to print the translations of Mercè Rodoreda in this issue. The poems are drawn from the second edition of Mercè Rodoreda, *Agonia de llum*, ed. Abraham Mohino Balet (Godall Edicions, Barcelona). Copyright © Institut d'Estudis Catalans

This issue has been set in Arno Pro, with titling in Argumentum. The flyleaf is set in Trend Sans.

Contents

In memoriam

Maurice Scully
1952–2023

Melissa Buckheit

Requiem: Myself from Me—Abiquiu, NM

Me from Myself – to banish – / Had I Art – / …
How this Be / Except by Abdication – / Me – of Me?
        —Emily Dickinson

It was like looking at oneself
from inside a grave

where you are
inside

but removed from your body

and instead looking in
to the thick divot, a cavern in sand.

I was not myself

and yet I was — I was
a ghost of a self

I had been many years or centuries ago

and in a sudden flash flood
of meaning

or natural means

I'd died in this exact space
in the sand

the limestone carvings
and diatomaceous earth

which crumble to touch.

5

In *Plaza Blanca,*
what was once ocean

before it was Ice Age
is in reverse.

Small skulls of rats
miniscule femurs and tibia were strewn

in the cavern.

I knew myself there
could see my corpse

doused in wet and dirt

like the rats who became of the cliffs a part,
a design, embedded.

I knew my hair strewn
from wind and rain

my lungs filled with sand, water
the alveoli full to bursting.

It was a beautiful thing

because nothing could be done.
I may not have been clothed.

These are the deaths that continue
and do not end.

Looking at myself
from elsewhere, not in my body

as if I were in a grave

I knew it to be true—

I could barely feel my flesh,

and all the things I had once held
were dead

but easily so.

For I had no tie to them
nor had they tie to me,

the cycle was complete.

The life I'd lived
and had met in this one—

it was done.

Pastoral: A Brief Driving Tour of New England Lands

i. Provincetown

here, on the edge of this coast, a coast of seashores which curls to a hook,
brushed and brush of sea grasses, fingers of an anemone

there is the body, blue reflector to the light, emanating, repeating, a silver
wave steeped in the fog, a white puff of cloud rising along the line of the
coast

it is silent, as if sound were something that only exists absent from water

I arrive and pull over in front of the sign reading, "Cape Cod National
Seashore" on a small triangle of sand at the turn in the road

it seems the end of the Earth, everything white with the humidity of sea,
how one can simply drive down the curl of land straight into the ocean,
Race Point or Herring Cove—

ii. Barnstable

in a rented car, winter, the slide of gravel beneath tire

no one is alive but what moves on this beach—
sand and wind, seaweed, tide, and gulls
  a few in the 'scape

  there is a thin film of gray, a translucent curtain:

  orange clam boots, muddy coast
          salted dogs hot and cold from Frisbee
    and a chase

they are the background, more gulls

the foreground   fat, living rocks against the mottled

and one eye, a tilting buoy

or the lighthouse which follows the shoreline
                                        in night hours

iii. East Greenwich

East Greenwich, in a rented car with my girlfriend, to exit to the Main Street

built just yards from the ocean and harbor, one can look down

the uneven cobblestones past the bank-parking to the sea, a steeper drop

than I remember from childhood
                                        the Atlantic is grey-blue-brown

in Rhode Island, omnipresent and familiar the sky is grey-white-blue

and interior beneath the surface

—clams, bright green reeds along endless salt ponds, gray fences—

every wood house worn with salt and wind, Colonials and Capes

every face worn a confluence

iv. Provincetown

long, mild, green, unending bar of the ocean below a tableau of blue

is the Atlantic in April off a coast of sand and mud, 40 miles—

you look out to sea and there is nothing or seems nothing near

but the relentless power of water in the pull of tides and current

pounding, a yellow sand and littoral flora in the constant wind what is the beauty of unbroken land claimed as protected shore

and its border of mudded, grassy cliff, peaking and breaking

following in parabolas asymmetrical

that to gaze you know the place

as it was just after an ice age

which is a feat

still the Pilgrims wintered in Provincetown Harbor

you see it written "where they first alighted on foot" or "took their
        first sip from a spring"
and what is such a thing and what is sacred and to whom

for you are here because of them in truth

even as these same lands formed by the words of other peoples earlier
        are unwritten

on signs like "First Encounter Beach" south past Eastham

like an essay toward a thing original, but completely unmentioned

how language both is and isn't enough while all that is held after is this water

so we explore the dunes and a broken industrial bunker closeted away—

opposing ends—world war, the named world, loss, the geological
        now evidential—

and we walk as Thoreau did but less, imperfectly, even painfully in deep sand

held by the glass sky and zinc clouds

Sophia Nugent-Siegal

The Torments

I — Reality

Nothing could be decently hated except eternity.
        —Giuseppe Tomasi di Lampedusa, *The Leopard*

There is nothing to be afraid of that is not an idea
We cling to flesh
As a dead deer does to a hook in a still life
Behind the slicing hand of the butcher
Lies the slicing hand of the painter
And beyond the artificer
Lies the truth—*death*

It is not the white of the bone
The battle-colour of the vein
Or even the shadows fallen upon the brain

It is the really existent extinction of existence
The Chaos perhaps
Which is not deep water
Only ideas stand sickle-handed
At the foot of made beds

And so we cling to flesh
Which alone is subject

II — Agony

... human appetites are insatiable, for since from nature they have the ability and the wish to desire all things and from fortune the ability to achieve few of them, there continually results from this a discontent in human minds and a disgust with the things they possess. —Niccolò Machiavelli, *Discourses on Livy*

Men are in love with the future and married to the past
Out of this the little mermaid's knives were forged
Life – the light on the white wall –
Is missed between wave and pulse

The stroke of the painter
The stroke of the demon's whip
And the lover's finger tracing out the chin

All the stars we dance under are dead
Clipped flowers wreathe the maiden's head
And her hair is parted by the sword
The planets flutter like swallow's wings
Defective in point of eternity

And I see a girl striking
The stream dragging it
Back to the past
Shattering her own reflection

III — Vision

Everything we have, everything we think we have, is taken away from us.
—*Battlestar Galactica*, season 4

Your heaven is my hell, my Cardinal,
For truth is the essence of pain
And pain is an illusion of the affections

She found truth in the apple's worm
In the imperfection we call a horizon
The black notional between blue and blue

I possess nothing but this idea of division
Which is the gift of the discernment
Of spirits
For seeing is incredulity

There are no caterpillar princes
And thus there is no Lucifer if you see him

Yet to know the truth is the essence of terror
To see white in its whiteness
Or even as it burns the green
Is to lose the last dark part
Of the red brain
Into which I should never have looked

M. Stasiak

These are your moments

Alannah,

I know the cancer is industrial in its efficiency
and you've been hooked and wired in white rooms
while those you didn't recognise came and went,
came and went,

                    and I know

the desperate horror of your impending death,
the wrongness of your life's arc ending at 19, but

                    don't do this. Don't

ask them to hang you in canisters of chemicals
in a Utah edge-of-nothing industrial estate and
keep you there, on contract, in a temperature-
controlled warehouse

                    as back at home

your mother dies, your father dies, your sisters
die, your nieces nephews and their children die
and you become a strange inheritance, a strange
responsibility that no one wants.

                    You need to understand

the cancer kills you. You're not preserved alive
and curable but as a corpse, the medics pushed aside
and company technicians rushing in.

Please think again. Allow

a tender ordinary heartbreak, here in your home, your
town, your piece of trodden ground near wooden
benches where your friends sit comfortless with grief.
Age with them in memory,

for this is your time,

your line, your cross-hairs in history. These are your
moments, that have cradled you since birth
and love you still.

Your own elsewhere

We are all in our own
elsewhere, grown up in
broken darkness,
desperate to locate
the lives we missed.
But time is facing just
one way. You cannot be
in San Francisco, 1969.
You cannot have
what you deserve –
childhood reconvened
with kindness,
and those you belong to.
They're lost, unfindable
right now. Somewhere
through endurance
lies your life.

We are all in our own
elsewhere, begun afresh
on the thinnest of

surfaces, scrambling
to shape our fate.
But DNA is facing just
one way, rocking us over
the third-floor carpark parapet
or into a gifted calm.
Life denies you. It
fritters away the dead,
withholding those
who might have been
your allies, who might have
held your corner in the
lifelong playground
punch-up you were born for.

Deep in your own sad past,
the incubated baby was
stripped of history
stripped of the womb.
Your life was facing
just one way, through
tiled rooms and into
the hands of strangers.
We need to tell a story
we can live with
and you must be black sheep,
endeavouring the dark
until each unrepented un-
forgiven dawn.
The jealous void has
kept you for its own, and
we are much older now.

It's all so far away,
like a fairytale, like the
child of faded parents
in a scrapbook,
like an ancient dream

compelling us to hunt hunt
to find out
how we were, and
who we were, then.
Those never meant to live
become immortal.
You take us tumbling
through space, and in the end
we see it. The universe
is facing just one way.
Seconds leak to eternity –
we follow them.

Note – In physics, happenings that cannot lie in the future or past of a particular event are said to lie in the 'elsewhere' of that event. What happens in the elsewhere cannot affect or be affected by anything in the past, present or future of the event.

Obsidian's cousin

The surface of the earth
                            supports us
springs us
                    buoyant with messages
out of the chemical fluxing night.

Breezes haul from
                    arms of the crossroads
we never took.

Absurd existence   falls back into gravity.

The minerals acknowledge us
                            obsidian's cousin

made of the same material
joined with the same desire

and scampering over the surface
                    like phosphorus flame.

Only life
            burns up this quick

thin blue light and   then the sudden dark.

At the edges of territories
where cliffs, cranes, horizons
                        all align, hear it –

the roaring
            strung magnetic stream
universe and moment given voice.

            We're staggered back
                        in solar wind, wrapped

around by spinning time

            dizzy, dazzled, joyous.

Aidan Semmens

Journal of another plague year

I

For all our sins, this body
is silent and secret now,
the poem a dying art
encrypting the dead
for Death hath many thousand slain
in this pestilence. Danses macabres
amid the interminable dying,
smells of cold sweat and old plaster
in chantry chapels –
division between the crypt
and the archive, stuffed
with our mortality

ruin, exile, loss
and the fall of heroes.

Evolution's path inexorably turned
by the random interruption
of asteroid collision;

transfer of earthly power
you may call political –
but on such scales
what is the choice
of one more Fukushima?

II

You were already so long dead to us
when you began to live the dream,

November now coming in like a quandary
of new leaves among the old,
illuminated from within, gold and green,
strange scents of fungus
stencilled in the morning air,
life springing from an axis of decay.
A crow treating a gravestone as an anvil
on which to hammer open an acorn,
an early morning thrush goading
the robin into song. The happy sound
of children in the plague-ground,
unmistakable in any language.

Young girls with pushchairs
on the riverwall at the lowest tide,
the hawk that spooked the redshanks
seen off by persistent rooks,
unrepentant cyclists spraying mud.
After months a fallen tree
finally cut through,
willows by the stream
making good their riposte
to last year's brutal slashing.
Half-vacant parade-grounds
villainously masked.

Don't toss, but place, the ball in the air
then throw the racket through it.
Having said that, it's the media,
a PR stunt. I mean it's nice, but
I didn't know you'd lived in Africa.
And I've got nothing to say but what a day,
how's your boy been?

I shall have to look this up because
I've got a big book on all the trees
and different things. Please
leave room for me to open my boot.

III

Ribald graffiti of a Nordic era
scratched out and overwritten
by generation after generation
of earlier cultures only guessed at.
Carcases of expired saloons
left out to rot in neolithic fields.

An ancient language with no future tense,
exoskeletal as the shell of a crab,
with shapes of fretting, stillness and erosion
carrying their own weight of meaning –
metaphor extended into epic
of memory and forgetting, misremembering
discovered as revelation.

Narrow village streets as deserted
as if struck by plague, fields and hillsides
abandoned to the sun – lives entombed
in rocking coffins on a wild sea
where nothing is possible but revolt
if only revolt were possible;

the deprived deprived even of sanity, led
towards a hell of their own construction
by madmen who feign
even their own madness, led beyond even
where a parasitic media corps will go,
a plastic paradise turned purgatory
for the lawyers, reality stars and other crooks
with nowhere else to go and going nowhere.

This septic isle tangled
in motif of the serpent, seductive curves
and alluring danger, shifting shapeliness and poison
undulating through the elliptic seascape;
mythologies of the littoral –

wave reflecting on shore, ocean becoming land,
land blending into sea, constant reshuffling
of topic and texture, sand into rock, rock into sand.

Maps of every scale redrawn, rewritten
for the unseeing, an illiterate library distilled.
Once I misinterpreted a snake as a coil of hose
or the inner-tube of a tyre until
it raised its head to look at me. The living snake
writhing in the hands of dancers as represented
in the electric firebreathing lightning bolt,
the gentle impression of ripples on a beach.

IV

It's approaching the Lewknor turn
puts me again on the road to Diamond Harbour,
title or starting point of many an unwritten book.

An icy fog materialises among the branches,
falls from the trees like rain,
like the eruption of Vesuvius in wartime,
lava overwhelming eighty US planes.

Frost in the shadows,
emerging into early sun,
rises as vapour. A dreamlike realism
overlays recollection
of walking through the empty city,
footsteps echoed back
from famous buildings, banking houses
and construction sites abandoned
for a day – or forever?

Obsessive tracing of bloodlines
as integral to this internetworked world
as pornography or

deep hidden military origins
might lead us to this darker place,
a site of innocence in a remote elsewhere;

here an occluded personal history
heads to a conclusion
which will solve nothing.
In this semi-urban cemetery
an ill-advised tree of heaven
is giving the nearby graves hell,
the stones' text moving,
blistered and obliterated;

these walls, these appended
homes and stockyards, half derelict,
you might choose to call beautiful
the rust in the standpipe standing
for whoever now knows what,
the paint peeling from the peeling paint
layers on the sills of eyeless windows –
its future now all yours.

Grim filmic tics like
'you'll have your eye out, kid',
which seemed a surreal joke
until the day Mags
or rather her infant son
dislocated her eyeball from its socket,
from which ever after
it was prone to slip.

In comical, commercial times like these
you might feel
Hades needs no legendary entrance
in a real cave geologically carved
by the action of water on limestone.

The road to Wellville's
paved with good intentions.

V

If I read Herodotus rightly,
it begins again with a god beheaded,
a begging bowl filled with ecstasy.
Angels assume bodies to appear to mortals;

a futile update by church bell and town clock,
breviaries and books of hours,
books of houris,
wall-paintings and manga,
various grotesque marginalia –

archangel Michael slaying the dragon,
one curious superstition
putting another to the sword.

We bring the ancestors trailing behind us,
bodily panic the unspoken subtext
of the tyrant, power of the masculine absurd.
We are not done with the death drive.

A heart weighed against an ostrich feather
in the Book of the Dead, daggers embossed
with images of wild beasts,
Homeric heroes and Shinto priests –
rough mosaics in the shape of dragon,
flowers and phoenix, statues
of gods in casual clothing
seeking consolation
in more ancient beliefs.
Seraphs are elsewhere
described as snakes, cherubim
with uncertain quotas of limbs and wings.

Dense foliage entangles the temples,
our believed and fictive lives entwine,
strangled in jungle vines
engaging the sad fragility of human things.

Hell's gateway's opened, disgorging
unexpected spirits to roam
for one night only, find the places
most convenient for ghosts
when the fires have died
and the streets are deserted.

In a modern utopia
of technologies that regulate urban space
the disembodied flow of 'information'
breeds anxieties of isolation
and social distance, listless toleration
of intolerable things.
In our refuges of domestic privacy

all our anger coalesces
round the foul graven image
of one patrician politician:
a man sentenced to death
will not much worry
about the running of theatres.

In the great inoculation
who gets the blood of the cow
and who gets a scrape
of a sufferer's pus?

Last year hell held more
than its common population of souls.

VI

Like a bad novel I am constructed
around an emptiness, an absence. The moment
just before waking of realisation
that your companions in this adventure,
whether welcome (parents) or less so (ex-spouse)
in the non-dreaming world are dead.

Totemic figures, shrunken heads and sculptures
ferried to the museum, the gallery

the massacres and the years of slavery, the deaths
and routine cruelties are become the dream;

Saint Roch with his plague sores and his dog
bringing succour and pestilence to the people.

The oldest human footprint outside Africa
exposed then erased by action of the sea: you must
look quickly to see as through a distorting mirror

a contingent and marginal existence
built over; and over and over. Branches
on an inverted tree, scraps and fragments,
hunting hyena and lion, the cave bear best taken
in hibernation, mammoth when you can,
smashing bone for marrow –

higher seas in a warming world
where badgers prey on turtles, aurochs
roam with beaver, boar and deer.

Mycelium's neural network
underpins everything, severing
pathways, making new – the ant
compelled to climb to its doom,

the saint, the human,
the holy sinner urged
against conscious willing,
where?

Carrie Etter

What Return

I walked into the woods the further reaches of the campground to the lake Dawson Lake was I seven or ten.

I read all the Laura Ingalls Wilder books and tried to make acorn meal which tasted bitter as a broken aspirin on my tongue.

I walked into the woods, toward sunset.

I walked away from my parents and younger sisters, sure of my return, sure of their contiguity, never imagining the moment from which I'd write.

I walked away from the Steury pop up camper, off-white with olive stripes.

What do you walk away from when you're seven or ten?

I walked toward the setting sun.

I look up the old Steurys on the internet. What would you pay to sleep inside the age of seven or ten, on a four-inch foam mattress in the squall of cicadas?

Burgundy

Not the likeness, the abrupt insistence on blood,
no, an extrapolation, from consciousness to the material world,

if you could portray such teeming – and perhaps
Rothko has – this dark stain

sometimes aloft, one band of sunset,
a falling maple leaf, sometimes a swathe of velvet,

not heart-colour so much as presence,
the smell of the air as you walk under winter sun or

poplars after rain, green musk,
the distillation of a heady

into now, into sight, and so perhaps,
perhaps indeed heart.

Purple False Foxglove

Here now into the corolla for the faint touch of

Such a flimsy, no hardiness to it

Let the bees have a heady month

Near the sandflats, near Lake Michigan

If flimsy, if frail, if tawdry, if a pale brightness

Who's to tell the girl otherwise?

Anise Hyssop

Admittedly I exhibit
a certain passivity.

Thronged by sun, by rain,
by six types of bee –

yet another proboscis
tickles....

Come July, I am whorls
of a hundred flowers, a hundred

purple mouths,
each bearing five teeth,

and oh if they could
bite –

On the Eve of a Second Lockdown

Look here the rough and tumble daisies and the pale yellow walls
call the colour sunlight or butter or the wine we drank in Rome one summer
and to remind us of that sky here are tall periwinkle curtains
and the bed appears a calm blue pool where we'll float on our backs
and look a fridge fresh squeezed orange juice and milk and marmalade
and on the counter a jar of coffee a bottle of wine a cafetiere a corkscrew
shall we call it our island on the island as we're in dear need of whimsy
in our call-it-not-a-cage in these shortening darkening days
come on put your nose in a flower tell me it smells sweet

Stuart Cooke

Coastal, as in Galactic

The moon is the first thing to notice, the first
to discard. We lean into a dark universe,

our legs blur beneath us, soon we can see it
from afar: our lost friends, our dying cities,

even the death of us. Some are playing
like glittering pistons, while many

wail like open ovens. The limbs
of a poet are woven from the letters

of a nova, dumb and magnificent as any
convoluted scale. If we journey into the flesh

to where our rhythm was lost, presence
spins into a gourd, continents into chords,

into chords; melodies of ecologies
are strobed into disco, I want

to groove with you, groove with you,
the madness of the music is a planet,

the harmony is a web, we are strung into desires
that exceed us, there is a halo around the hole

in the centre of our allotment.
When I step out of the documentary

I'm confronted with a quadrant, I build a haiku.
Inside the poem I am safe, I play a trombone,

my life begins when it leaps,
I jump and we're alone. Only a painting

could frame your thicket. I want record
of my adoration, I will scrawl in dance.

When presence becomes impression I burst
with collective, our crowns of forest ignite;

I coat my cells in the ocean's crumbed plastic,
where is the right position?

But we crowd into the negative, we fade
into the valley of the voice. Has the story already

come to an end? Where
were we going? Feeling that progress toward

infinity had crystallised in us, that we in fact
were the other we had been awaiting, and any glance

over the shoals of possibilities
that lay strewn by our globular record

was like gazing into a mirror reflecting the inner-
most depths of the soul… Often the truth is a lie,

the word conceals a mob. Discarding
the void of Mind, I wade into the muck

between the marks, the interval mutters,
I press upon another, entangle with its

mass; to speak is to move, to bend, to be;
we tell as we are told, on a stage of gesture,

touch, retreat. I will finish the circle,
I will abandon narration, oration,

the body will lose its tone; let me hear you by horn,
by failure, by flight. We are rush hour

along the freeways of a dying thesaurus,
the will is the music that frames us,

the body disappears when it stops.

Wollombi

For Martin Harrison

Hauling my phantom across the fields,
my voices lilt in the anonymous hours.
Summer sweats with crumbs of spring.

A lake trembles in the breeze
in a bruised, shallow valley
with a worn polish of pasture.

Woodlands stitch the sky.
Orange-flecked boulders
are strewn between wood and word

like ancient marks of punctuation.
After silence
cicadas rattle my engine, flatten Yengo;

the present disappears. Over the wrangled fence
of the badlands, down into the wound,
solar flares stripe a furry rump, a dappled patch

choked by pine clutch—
there you are, wisping into a premonition.
Entombed in the glade, what I expect

bumps into what I feel.
The ground thrives with sugar ants.
The grass is greener over your grave.

Jaime Robles

Five Poems from *Fire*

An ember nestled in the bowl
Of cupped hands.

Blow on it and the green lands
Before speech flame into being.

And fire, released
Collides with the air above.

§

Those clouds that should be intermediaries
Soaring across a flat blue sky toward heaven
Belong to earth

Flame caught between unreachable heaven
And earth

Does heaven mean the sky
I imagined I could reach up and touch?
A divine land? Or far space.

Clouds radiant with light
Trees crowned with blossoms of bright fire

§

A finger raised in a whisper
The heart follows its movement
Pointing
To the sky above

Fingers fold into each other
Drop from prayer
To the earth and then rise

Connecting the temple
The eye

Thought follows the body's flame

§

Within the darkness
The man leans in
Slowly to
Breathe in the fragrance
Of the woman beneath him

Settles in
Like heat

Fruit of fire

spinning into thousands –
lamps of pure flame on twigs hung loosely

§

She frames her face with her open hands –
The moon, her fingers the feathers
Of wings, one on each side

Light
Murmurings
Ash
A field of small gestures

Nathan Shepherdson

paintings would return
for Gil Jamieson 1934–1992

I.

paralleled by the manifesto
that he would be dead by 30
he continued to move away
from the categorisations of art
to art that always spoke for itself,
always urged people to reach
inside their own interpretations,
one to one, in landscapes
constantly wrestled with paint,
he found himself as a ten-year-old,
emphatically predicted to approach
figurative thought with subtle movement,
in a formulated tenor, doing National Service,
to acknowledge a myth, never prepared,
a rheumatic sketch surfaced among artists,
in nudes documenting political sincerity
following expectation into its sonnet family,
to farm Antipodean experience,

II.

he returned with grandiose plans,
and we set off again, to paint
a giant mirage, with both relationships
as a major influence, best displayed
in the killing he sought an escape from death,
to depict survival he painted raw truth,
and continued to exhibit there, in deep respect,
he returned to earlier times

because his mother was sick
because his mother commenced
a touring phase in his life,
commenced a close friendship
with famous art patrons, most impressed,
fishing for hard life over a waterhole
at Three Moon reflected upon the idea
first shown to exhibit cruelty,
he returned to exhibit 360° insanity
to depict both auctioneers after the sale,
exclusive drought dodgers from the coast
eating piglets on his land

III.

paintings would return as self-portraits
as his contemporaries were achieving
a remoteness from criticism, he consoled
himself on canvas, to try to start painting
again, after open heart surgery,
after family tragedy, in 1985,
his mortality precipitated an intimate
association that never compromised
the non-second living near himself,
befriending himself, in the Five States,
that never sold readily, his second mortality,
again, managed to paint 30 self-portraits,
while he was hung in non-acknowledgement,
in a hospital with its archaeologist owner,
down south, a great supporter, down south,
to think a number received into himself
to receive art as himself into a number,
Bushman time dogmatic about not being Establishment time
in and around closer areas,
in and around the one representative,
in and around advanced diagnosis
he began travelling further

to move the cliff to the cancer
painting the education of time,
these paintings formed the new crop,
in great volumes producing song
in figurative oils never completed
his self-portraits bought themselves
in June 1992 in Monto
his self-portraits paint themselves
in Monto.

Note: this sequence was constructed from words contained in the Matthew Jamieson essay *A Painter of the Land*. (*Life on the Land* – Rockhampton Regional Gallery 1997).

upstares
for E

two speakers say nothing
when the work is
untitled

and money on the table won't burn
until they find a match (between)
the two thoughts on offer

a white cloth hastily draped
over the body of a pun
is (still) amusing

in the car on the way back
from the gallery you tune the radio
to yourself

and tell me, 'poets are born ghosts,
only become people
when they die'

Cole Swensen

Buried Rivers

A river running under is that much stronger, its pull on the surface largely unnoticed, the current perhaps more electrical than physical, yet still so effective. For instance, the Bièvre still runs under Paris, centuries after Rousseau walked along it (The Sixth Walk) collecting plants on the Gentilly side. And some two hundred years later, Louise Bourgeois leapt into it to escape her father, which didn't work. So they paved it over and named it the rue de Bièvre. It's an odd street to walk along because somehow you find yourself at the end much sooner than you'd have thought.

A river buried is always hurried – is always a burning – some century of scattered candles. Like the electricity that activates a muscle – turns fluid and a flame follows its fuse to the sea.

Paper Boats

A friend is telling me about a festival in his hometown; it's called the Bali Jatra, and it celebrates the day that all the merchants were all expelled and fled to Bali in the 11th century. I'm impressed by what seems to have been an early anti-capitalist gesture that's still being celebrated a millennium later. And the residents honor it by launching intricately folded paper boats out across the river.

In my mind, they're always lighted – an origami flotilla precise in candelabra, gliding off and glowing amber – though clearly not from candles, as the lights don't flicker and the boats don't burn down, and yet, I've never been able to figure out where the light comes from.

Though, actually, it turns out that I'd remembered it all wrong – it is called the Bali Jatra, but, in fact, it's a celebration of the establishment of trade with far distant lands. And they do launch paper boats, and they are lit up, but there's no mystery about where the light comes from– each boat carries a little candle, and given the nature of fire and paper, sooner or later, they do all go up in flames, becoming floating torches, each a tiny riot on its way outward, and the children on the banks clap and shout and laugh and wave good riddance.

Amy Evans Bauer

sound field

how
you echo

field sound
who
you echo

sounds feel
now
you, Echo

how sounds
each
brown cow

sounds cow
brown
eacho

sound cow
browns
field

I cow
round
udders filled

you cow
downs
full field

I return
to woods as
boom

wave & wave
hit
cow & cow

I permitted
this return
me dow dow

no dowager
exo
field felt

empty
middle circled
where

lost babes
don't sing:
all fell

down
my vib's
my own

mid ripples
of unploughed
field as

not of
pond
flames

lit to
sunk lady
afire

—*August 2022*
Tan House Banks, Sevenoaks, UK

notes on horsey beach

silent gull
over

ghost
vowels

that bond
shes and pups

in three
weeks across

wet years—
haul

weight of two-
kilo days

to fatted
ocean

out and
in

.

numerous autumn
clutters beach

with pinnipeds'
bulk—

watched rocks
who howl

at moon
whiskered

with pelt
and fang—

bodies' moans
outsing

sea's
curves,

throw minims
to wind

in love
haunt

—October 2021

Mary Leader

Alternative Canticle of Mary

Diminuit anima mea Dominum
~

My soul diminishes
   the Lord.
  Too late
ever again
   to turn my forehead
  to the sky
with my eyes
   closed to receive
  what?

~

My purview consists
   wholly of wheel-gouged
  roads, whether
the gouges stream
   as if sick with flood,
  or, like eye-slits
in merciless sun,
   bake, bandageless
  and blind.

~

No awareness
   of my importance exists,
  save for a carved
M
   inside one utterly
inaccessible cave:
  my unique mind.

~

I did ask
                God for it, for that
        miscarriage.
Asked by rescinding
                pointblank, my availability
        as vessel.
What could God even say?
                No way could he complain,
        since it had been made it clear to me
that my heartfelt
                consent was of
        the essence.

~

Stupid girl.
                Blithe, stupid girl.
        I spared
a human-to-be
                the crux of
        a death-to-be.
I spared myself
                what I believed
        at the time
was the very worst
                pain possible
        on this earth.

~

Childbirth? Hardly.
                Pain from the inside
        out.
Beyond worthless rags,
                beyond old but decent
        towels,

good clothing
                    ripped up
          as more blood
and more and
                    more of it exceeds
          serviceable fabric.

          ~

Conceivable violence
                    much worse than childbirth:
          to stand powerless
there
                    as the flesh of my flesh
          grows up to encounter
evil
                    incarnate
          and equipped.

          ~

To stand there
                    without adequate language, without
          any language, as their screams rend
all the air.
                    Whipped, raped, burned, head
          held under water.
Fingers, ears, lips, easily removed.
                    Tenderness, flayed.
          Castrated. Mocked.
Height, attained in line with forebears,
                    suspended, unsupported
          above the ground, or

          ~

Or buried within the ground
                    up to the neck as

47

```
        stones
hurled overhand
                in increasing frenzy
        strike
the face
                the scalp
        the scalp again
again the face
                again again
        the cranium.


~


Avoided, personally.
                Even so,
        stupid decision.
Stupid
                but blithe,
        I tell you.
I did
                not feel
        momentous.


~


In my dotage, by touch,
                by compulsion,
        I collect
meaningless
                linen, meaningless
        parchment,
bread, wax, meaningless all,
                oil, dew,
        clay.


~


Forbidding myself
                to pray, I make
```

of kinds of rock
a litany: ignorant, obsessive,
                adamant; rubble
        in chunks, projectile;
slabs of sapphire, tablets
                of the law; gigantic boulder
        rolled across the mouth
of the sepulcher,
                meant to prevent wild animals
        or marauders
getting hold of
                a body not yet completely
        prepared for burial.

~

Yet neither that barrier
                nor a sweet
        certain face
is there, there
                to be, in passing,
        glimpsed.
No beloved hand
                gestures,
        passing.

~

Less. No
                search
        is undertaken.
I come forth,
                having foreclosed
        miracle, having
precluded resurrection,
                proceed to the true
        worst pain possible:

~

49

Knowledge
                    that in the official chain,
      I'd have outlived
the third-worst pain,
                    the second-worst pain, any pain
      mine or the child's,
and on this earth;
                    I would have been able
      triumphantly to say:
Now, I stand up and depart,
            for the word I conceived
      is not in this grave.

~

What now
                would I give?
      Would? That word
is rubbed out.
                There is nothing
      nothing I could
give
                for five minutes
      in the time before:

~

Young mother-a-common,
                taking healthy
      feet for granted,
walking the pathway
                of her secret
      fecundity.

Martin Anderson

from 'River Water'

Autumn

   Under frost
white boughs   foot
       steps
through ochre
              leaves
  powder. Words

   are expendable.
Look.
        A bird sings.
   Listen.
       Night
's never far off.

Common Roads

   The plucked string
      vibrates.
      Who
plays upon us.
           Taut
    bodies under
    sun wind rain

          sing

   bones
are never quiet.

Winter

A cold wind blows
through the window

Smell of withered flowers
        Someone
is walking talking
                    in their sleep

    repeating a question

at the corner of the street
        a huddle
    of snow & shadow
                    a life

worn down

Silence

                    Poetry
        porous little parsimonious
                            possession
        abates.
                Stone cold.
            Mnemosyne.
                        Your lips
            are grey
        curses heaped
        upon the dead.
                    Say:
    "I will not crook the hinges of my back
    for five pecks of rice a day."

Words

Drifts pile up
        avalanche
of discarded   words
                        discard
themselves.
            What accumulates
        soon dissolves
inference and all structures through
    which identities rise
                        signs
        of anxiety.

    Trying to cut water.

            Water
    dissolves words.

River

            The curdled sound
                in the ear
                    Cries
            "Look   Listen."

                            Pale green buds
                            across the river.

    If you can reach them.

Eliza O'Toole

Wind force & found feathers
(Tyro alba)

it was the part, the broken part
it was the anatomy of an owl

it was slow flight, long and low
it was wing loading and low aspect ratio

it was inner weathervanes and fringes
it was trailing edges,

it was silent flight

it was the glide, the velvet slide,
the grooves and camber line, it was
the chord, the bow, the hook and the elliptical decline,

it was inaudible, it was free stream loading
apart from boundary layer at reduced velocity,
vortices arising, it was the formation of a separation bubble
it was shear stress

it was shaft and vane, calamus and rachis
proximal barbules and bow radiates, it was distal
and it slid soundlessly, its airframe attenuating
large eddies shed from blade and leading edge
serration

it was sound, a scattered
attack corresponding to a stall

the owl wing, it was very thin
just a single layer of primary feather

it was the trailing edge and leading fringe
it was a hollow call

it was the elbow of the owl

A little about gall & leaf rolling

it was that, the sound of the rain but no rain
it was that, the slough of skin, the hollow nave, the scattering of things

the silken sticky thread, the bark sown just so
the moss silvered and slithered, the pin feather, May flies and
hagabon, the susurrations of the three barn owlets
and leaf rollers defoliating the oak

it was that, first foliar flush, it was its green, obscene
lime lit from behind before the fall and diapause
it was an eclosion, bud-break & *semiferanus* instar spinning
rolling folding tying leaves webbing it all together

hanging by threads, folded into the bark, grub rubbing

it was the gall wasp, round honeydew
release of sweet phloem exudate, ooze and dripping
and bacterium, it was that
Erwinia quercina, dripping different galls
on different parts at different times indifferently

it was that, it was beaked
twigged rusty red with yellow spots, it was
metamorphic and the oak, in lull, chordwise
and spanwise

was metaphoric and is now pedunculate

it had clean wings, modified leading edges
it was that, and it defoliated the oak

after-ripening

after auxin, pattern formation
a taproot sets in the garden
first a hypocotyl and two cotyledons
all folded over as the embryo grows
seed coated and midheartened

then turning green, torpedoes
oiled and waxed toward germination
either seedling lethality or apical lineage
dependent expression of allelic tissue
patterned and lodged in the meristem

the soil smells of damp Labrador and blood
the impress of me uprooting trees
old and cold remembering
heavy rain wintering ground with pellucidity
where hollow wings boned once keened
in an ash grey snow lightened sky, then with elongation
root to shoot, canonises time transcribed radically
by RNA methylation

Amlanjyoti Goswami

After Carl Spitzweg, in five parts

1. The Bookworm (1850)

I was looking for that one about the flying habits of the dodo, circa 1743, written by a French Monsieur Pierre something but all the libraries are closed and this is the best I have. I was thinking of calling Pierre wherever he is. Instead I have to settle with the Dreaming Habits of Bovine Forms 1776 which swats a fly or two and makes me ruminate but it is not the same thing. I must be getting late for breakfast.

2. The Intercepted Love Letter (1860)

I wondered whether to let it go or keep it up. In the end I decided to write one back. It said: 'Those on upper floors must step down to see the sun'. I waited. The tough one was wondering which one to catch, which to let go. Only the two pigeons knew who the lovebirds were.

3. The Poor Poet (1839)

The garret for measure, he checks his inner weather as the open umbrella comes near and the storm hastens the night breathing in gasps. The volumes nearby are collected works and he is nowhere around. He comes to grip with it when the feather in his mouth asks him to wait a little, open the window and let the sun in.

4. The Hypochondriac (1865)

To blame me for taking a deep breath outside is very historical. The plants green at my window, the bird feed above. I take in the air, there is little else to take. Elsewhere it is still night behind closed doors, someone stitching the two ends of a good life.

5. Gnome watching Railway Train (1848)

In time they will call my world dark. Magical. They will invent names for my sunset, my tree hollow. That thing steams ahead into the future, hurtling past my old haunts of myrtle and periwinkle. It has cleared the forest. Someday, they will miss this tree hollow, my footsteps and the murmur of water where I slake my thirst.

Sunset with the crows

The sun is about to leave.
Crows swerve past all attention
Then suddenly grow quiet.
Congregate at the neighbour's water tanks.

Five of them, on the roof
White water tanks, with things written on them
Things you cannot read. It is not clear
What the crows are doing there.

They are not drinking water.
They are not looking at water.
This is no crow-and-pebble-story of hard work.
The covers are intact. Water isn't dripping.

There are many crows, and one sunset.
The sun is all orange with desire.
The romantic in me – thinks, they are gazing at the sun.
But only I watch the sun go down.

No one else, between sun and me
These crows, in their bliss and strange communion.
They are just looking at each other
Oblivious of the sun.

Multicultural Reflections, Sunday Afternoon

The best I've had in years
Just next door.

Travelling around the world – and back,
Two minutes from home

In the nearby coffee (and ice cream) shop
Where the waiter taps ice bottle on wood,

For froth – like ambition- to settle down
And then fills some more, a scientist with a test tube.

How she spoons an extra scoop for you,
How she packs it for home.

Ah, but the jarring loud bhangra on speakers
Makes reading impossible, that book on exile poetry

But this is no dim lit café in Casablanca
As the waiter hums the bhangra tune, pouring coffee

Cold as ice cream, turning the volume down.
As a new one comes, speaking in halting angrezi

A foreign tongue, while the emperor sweeps the scene
In a single scoop.

I leave quietly, when she says they are open till 4 am,
& that people come only after dinner.

Rob A. Mackenzie

The Book

"And we tore dark squares, thick pages
From the Book of Fire" —George Mackay Brown, 'Peat Cutting'

The book dug into the dark beginning as a burning dog
      might chase its comet tail, white hot and haphazard
            in a cloud of steam, or a crowd kettled by the force

of blunt instruments, wag wag wag: the sway of it,
      the stagger, the collapse, the page turned in one
            mass semi-circular slump – thump! crash! – bodies

bellowing flame, but only yesterday the 26 bus
      looked like a beast surplus to the apocalypse,
            its windows smashed and tyres torn into spaghetti;

the book clothed itself with that bus and then
      undressed again, the world continued as it had
            ever been, the new normal cut in shattering glass,

the big bang, the freewheeling ride everyone
      says they want and then spends a lifetime trying
            to avoid, the book of inner life that's so fascinating

to no one whomsoever, certainly not to vandals
      throwing boulders at buses and ripping their knives
            into wheels to the honking laughter of land rovers,

honk! honk! honk! perhaps that was the vandals…
      they're all just one happy family in the book going
            up in smoke, the vandals and land rovers shooting

the shit together, whatever that means, it's like
      with like or perhaps like like with like, the level
            of simile, not reality, in the shush! the swish!

the pages turning, the pages of the book – shush!
      swish! – emporium of ideas that will never be any
            use to anyone, and whatever my story, the book

will tell it differently; it will catch up with the past
      before I know it, wordlessly – woof! woof! woof! –
            barking prophecies, entirely of events that have

already happened, as nothing hasn't happened
      already, and there is so much to discover in what
            we think we already have read within the bonfire

of information the book contained, which now
      feels uncontainable, spreading in disintegration
            like a dog's shadow escaping the confines of its dog,

dragged from its proper place by the kerbside
      or basket, silhouette sniffer now with palpable
            ambition to be an upwardly mobile status symbol

of freedom – badges! labels! photo-shoots! –
      worn lightly until lightly worn and then easily
            discarded like a slogan that has served its purpose

of buying in, like the inspirational Mandela
      fabricated quotation brought to you by Google
            with land rover pop-up and magic tree carrying

precise scents from Donald Trump's upper neck
      swiftly reclassified as illegal chemical weapon:
            stock for Novichok, radioactive soup for the soul-

less spirit; the book extends its sympathies,
      withdraws its condolence, proclaims neutrality
            and its impossibility, sits on the fence and falls

randomly on one side or the other, but always
      falls, takes the fence down with it, and leaves
            the hostile fighters drawing fresh dividing lines

to fight over: the broken shell of the 26 bus
   a meaningless boundary where they pitch
      boulders into territorial cairns, or like the dog

cocking its leg promiscuously at a scattering
   of lampposts; a similar excitement at being
      named in the book's microscopic footnotes,

less appendix than appendicitis, flared up
   and hosed down, emerging like a writer whose
      emerging is continual and perennially moot,

a mosquito buzzing distinctively from ear
   to ear, chapter to chapter, isolated even
      from subplots and tangents destined to be

dumped at first proofs, the book primed
   to re-establish the forgotten in ecstatic
      pulp briquettes, combustible biomass,

flames rising high but with lower grade
   warmth than the endlessly recyclable
      wooden traditions the book so loves

to run with, and then cut – thick pages
   globbed together, hellish papier-mâché
      gloopy oblongs, like plinths prepared

for abandoned statues, oyez! oyez! oyez!
   The town criers roar, *Is Language Dead?*
      in what might as well be an unknown

pre-Etruscan tongue rumbling from buses,
   as rocks are flung, the book scribbles on,
      and every era proclaims a golden age.

Carl Walsh

Viking lovesong

aloft, this banded whisk
ploughs sky
wind-eye shuttered
            /a loose kindling

the scant scale – a gap
an axle-whirl
            of want

I bask in the billow
this bleak gust knotted – a race
            athwart
through ribs of regret

Note: poem primarily composed of words that entered the English language from Old Norse.

I confess I'm teapot with curiosity...

The wind brays – I think of Joyce.
That he was 10 years younger than me
when *Ulysses* was published – two copies
for his 40th birthday. My copy, unread.
Slotted between pages – a torn out slip
of newspaper (remember them)
spruiks a writing prize, 2003. I'm pretty sure
I didn't enter. The wind winds around me.
I'm not sure why I think of Joyce now. Or think
that Nora Barnacle is a great name. Or that
Áine, who went to church with my mum, said
I should just open it randomly and read...

The title is part of a line from James Joyce's Ulysses *which turned 100 in 2022.*

in lockdown, remembering walking
Offa's dyke path, Wales 2002

I look at photos, they string together a being – remind me
of forgetfulness; of mortality. That log blooming with fungi

will have rotted into earth. That hill will still be Hergest Ridge, if
indeed, that's where it is. It only meant something because of Mike

Oldfield. As if, in an unintended homage to 70s rock, I hadn't just
slithered down a Black Mountainside. This church in some unknown

village still has its dead. A black and white Tudor house in full colour –
bulk of brick chimney. Solitary lamppost leaning in foreground, suspended

flow of roof tiles. The roadway patched and darned – a sign (which squinting
I still can't read). A rutted track coursing drunken – rectangles of hedgerows

intersect the frame. Google finds me 'Gladestry' – as if names only exist
in cyberspace deleted from cells of memory – this air drawn

into lungs, expelled into an afternoon – walked away from.

Michelle Penn

Stress questionnaire

Filtering: you were handed a promise/life on a silver platter but notice only the scratched surface.

Overgeneralization: the platter is scratched, therefore all beauty will be marred, all success conditional. Scratches like corridors leading only to more scratches.

Catastrophizing: spill the tea and a tsunami follows. Each mistake a high-walled box, you will be locked inside, the sky will taunt you with blue.

Black and white thinking: the platter must be perfect. There is nothing to be done with damage.

Labelling: the platter is face. The platter is skin. The platter is mind. The platter is voice. Desire. Potential. Weakness.

Mind-reading: everyone who sees you thinks you're damage, they sense it and step lightly around your name, as if it were a bomb.

Fortune-telling: the platter will always drag behind you, clanging, a lead swan.

Discounting the positive: a promise/life on a platter, but you prefer to make lemons from lemonade, spit out the apple to savour the worm.

Personalization: you are a colossus, a shadow on the light itself.

Should/ought: you should/the world ought. Leave the paper behind on a silver platter. What else is there to say?

Truth: a love poem

Truth is a swoon. It's the little wobble, the first stutter of the brain, a skid in the smoothness of vision. A Victorian heaving of a corseted chest. The vapours.

Truth, beauty, or something like that, in the old eyes. But in mine –

I know my name. I know the inheritance of hands.

Truth is a pyramid, inverted, its point teetering on the crown of my head and I'm balancing it, trying careful steps as it digs into my scalp. Or it's lambswool wrapped around a swollen toe. Or you can explain what it is and if not, offer more of your skin.

Picture of guilt as permafrost

The lesson imbibed like blood-milk woman weaned on weight passed through blood through milk flaws both hers and not accidents of history and birth veneer over every pleasure why are you worthy this ground frozen and unyielding lesson as landscape forbidding her from owning her own pain entire ice age of obdurate blood immovable milk accounts perpetually negative no idea who to pay she opens veins pumps her breasts dry still swallowing the lesson like a newborn thirsty trusting —

Petra White

The Mirror

1
Behind my master, I walk two paces
His fatherly rage sharp as the dew
that glitters between our toes,

his over-the-shoulder words
falling all around me like arrows.
The lake follows his ear-clipping voice,

I stand invisible in the dust and shadows,
a scarecrow almost loved.
His rage grows vital in my heart.

2
Behind my master, I walk two paces
The world aware it is ending
sheds tears of gold

that my master pockets for safekeeping.
For the next world, which God will create
out of burnt limbs, eyes,

pieces of our trouble. Everyone
in that world will glow with fierce sunlight
as I do in the shadow of my master.

3
Behind my master, I walk two paces
past and through
the salient world that lets us pass.

The kindly trees have eyes and pass judgements
under their leaves. My master says,
make sure you are a good testimony,

and grins at a tide of faces blank
as his gleaming teeth. I hold his long skirts
between thumb and forefinger.

4
Behind my master I walk two paces
He unspools me into eternity
I long for the skull of the Lord.

I dare not ask my master
whose faith is as firm as a shackle.
In the silent ballrooms of heaven

he alone sings lustily.
I keep eyes to the ground where white narcissi
weep around my feet.

5
Behind my master I walk two paces
He tells me I am almost perfect.
A velvety darkness swims

in my young eyes.
I am briefly struck blind.
The wind scrabbles at the glass night,

a voice trying to sing a long way off.
My master looks small
at the feet of his own shadow.

6
Behind my master I walk two paces
The sun roars and I long for pineapple.
All finite creatures of the earth

streak through my heart,
leaping to avoid their small deaths.
My master says, soon we will walk to our gold seats

in God's great kingdom.
I whisper to the Lord,
who pretends he cannot hear.

7
Behind my master, I walk two paces
He and I stumble alone
on the fields of a childhood.

My conduct is immaculate, like the not-
forgotten Spring. I drink with a silver tongue
from a little stream, fluent as a voice.

Weeping, he pulls me up by the collar.
The road ahead shines like a mirror
rushing infinitely towards us.

Leda one afternoon

What nobody knows is I kept
one of his feathers,
a souvenir, perhaps,
or warning.
I kept it for my daughter,
white feather weak as my fist,
as my body, that struggled
only as if with itself,
almost choking
in that whipstorm of feathers,
each one a word, that would clang
in my mind
down the years.

Like a clenched
fist unclenching
or a gust
dissipating, leaving motionless air.
Body pressed deep into the grass,
rivulets of blood
staining my legs.
I too became a bird.
Without wings,
yes,
without plumage,
bald as a hatchling,
raw-skinned, silent.

Of course I thought
of what would hatch
inside me,
the little birds
with mortal wings
and immortal eyes,
what would they see.
And what would I see
when I looked at them,
children
bathed in my blood.
How could I love them,
how could I not,
half and
wholly mine,
brimming
with the sun, its coldness.

Alec Finlay

from *some little shocks*

who knows the feeling:
you hear the door open
and are glad *and* afraid?

*

I love
to think of us

sharing meals
remember us

safe with a table
between us

*

for the violently enraged
their violence lasts a moment

for those exposed to their violence
every moment is alive

with the fear that rage
will reignite

*

"I don't know where
all this anger came from"
– *well then, learn*

*

fight or flight
     don't forget

her friend says
     freeze

*

the bag's packed
it's time to tell them
hid in the cupboard
it's time to be hit
that you're leaving
for the last time

*

no-one is responsible
     for anyone else's violence

everyone is responsible
     for how they respond to it

*

she put me
     back together

with care
     and cauliflower

*

after leaving you might
dream them kind again

Norman Jope

Art and Labour

for Ian and Ed

I stare at the façade of the Wedgwood Institute, counting dwarves at their exertions. It's impossible to work out what they're doing at this distance, even as I magnify the view. Some of Arthur Berry's 'lost pubs of Burslem' are still visible – unlike the lost hopes of Brexit – but the dwarves are confined to their parapet and cannot enter. The citizens are currently confined to streets and homes and cannot enter them either.

On Waterloo Road, there's a tree growing on the *inside* of a disused shop, next door to the derelict Taj Mahal restaurant. Perhaps, in time, it will burst through the roof and become a ladder to heaven. Or perhaps the outside is on the inside… and breaking down that door will return me to a garden I can never leave.

Everywhere, there are red walls… but that's only the colour of the local brick. In contrast, a grand opening of Caprino's Pizzeria is taking place, and has been taking place since October… a crescent-shape of lime-green balloons is festooning Market Square, accompanied by two employees in facemasks clasping their hands in hope.

From this vantage, the spliced-together villages extend for several miles. There's no clear exit from the warren, any more than there's a clear way down for the terracotta workers on the Institute's façade or the burly ghosts of vanished industries. The glazed-in tree keeps growing near the Afghan Palace takeaway and the Heaven and Hell nightclub, striving to return an exhausted urban agglomeration to the forest.

Faced with this scene of spliced-together days and years, I am less than a ghost and lose the power to judge. My art gives way to all the labour in this landscape, numberless hours of toil that leave dark traces on the map.

Seducing a Nun

after the film 'Ida' by Pawel Pawlikowski

She danced where she stood. I played
my exuberant saxophone and saw her –
Ida and Naima, poised yet ready
to lose control like the decade to come,
muse of the hallowed ground
of Eden revived. A few adventures later,
she was dancing in my arms
and then, naked, her hair unbound
like the possibilities of jazz,
she was under me and over me –
but I was the one to be renounced.
Fifty years later, her pebble glasses
and bent form passed me as I busked.

Growing Old in a Strange House

D'Annunzio at Il Vittoriale

Trinkets amass, and smart medallions.
I creep between statues draped with flowers
that are changed at least daily – perfumed as I am,
my trail's almost visible. Still, I court posterity
as a savage clown subverts my hopes from a distance.
My women remain young but their entrance fee goes up
each time, as I dress and undress them like dolls.
I've secreted this monument that masses around me,
assumed immobility so that it can't be imposed.
'Death tempts me', I write, but this is just three words.
I'm scared, just like the rest. I forget what I was doing
five minutes ago. And I've mislaid my laurel.
It's still on your head, says a voice from nowhere.

Daniel Hinds

Aneirin

> 'Gochorai brain du ar fur caer
> Cyn ni bai ef Arthur'
> —Y Gododdin

Aneirin, an air in furs let into a lordly place.
He staggers in with the wind.

Slips, and skins his palms and knees on the stones.
The last legend of a year-long pub crawl
Makes his entrance; moves from foot level to table,
Slides into the poet's trance.

The blue armour of his grieving stance:
Full height, eyes roving, feet still, a drink
Where his shook hands can reach.

Aneirin's skin is glass; in hall they see distorted
The stretched faces of the men behind him.

The froth and foam of a shake of the horse's lips
Settles a scum on a small gold lake.

Tongue forever slick with the wet of mead,
Loud and confident as a man drunk, he mourns.

Though he was no Arthur
Hands reached for him from the glass.

The hands hardy, burly, lordly, friendly,
Not the thin cold white of some unearthly lady.

He wore the bee's blood lather best and slid
Between the din, the trampling of men under iron-shoed
Men and the high screams of the horses.

His skin dappled in the white hives of the fearful,
His armour striped, yellow-black.

The taste of blood salt and mead sweet;
The vapour from his mouth plumes like the hovering souls.

If he were to give one more drop for each man
His mouth would go dry, his skin peel invisible.

He is a skilled barman; knows just how much to pour.
He flicks a settled fuzzy bug from the curving rim.

Only when he is done do they empty their glasses;
The drinking solution to all his problems.

Ravens pick at killed men and living insects.
The poet lives a honeyed life.

Squashed beneath the palm,
You find the dead insect smeared on goat hide.

Twice the Man

'stare / in a mirror long enough and he would come'
        —Gregory Leadbetter, 'Mirror Trick'

Under cover of the sound of sky, the neophytes gather
Where stone is coldest and the forest sleeps.

They bring out the long bowl.
They dollop bull's blood in pools at either end.
They breathe onto the mirror pane.

An old headmaster, the lines of shadow under his eyes
Like the subtle curl of a feather's black rachis,

Whose subject has fallen from the curriculum
Like his god from his kingdom, says the words,
Weighs out the Greek gramarye on his tongue.

Then they all look up.

They look up so long
Their age begins to tell.
There is not a Greek among them.

When the frayed bolt hits He is for a moment infinite.
He is for a moment infinite, in a way a man can be infinite,
Not in a womanly shape of eight asleep,
But in a single line stretching like a pillar
Glistering through earth and sky,
Time become a single number counting up in blue digital light,
Like a single sentence without a full stop,
A poetry that for all its complexity
And unbroken lineation cannot be understood.
He finds the hot forge at the core;
He puts on the lightning crown.
The thorn crown blinks, Allah winks out,
The countless Hindu deities go uncounted,
Sikh sheaths go empty and unsought, turbans unspool,
The circumcised go uncircumcised,
Budai's swollen belly is vexed and goes concave,
And highest throned Nothingness is filled.

All the holy books go blank and blue.

The raised eyebrows of the men disappear.
Clouds fill their heads. Too dark, too bright.

Shards split and catch the blue webs of their palms.

Juno, one cries, *Zeus*, spits the man, *Dyaus*;
They fight, and in the confusion another man dies.
Seared retinas flash with hot snapped silver knives
That show insides their insides.

The mirror goes black and cracks.
Light retreats into the high roiling depths.
The blade sticks in the head.

Steel is better than iron better than
Bronze better than lead.
But in a pinch an empty shine will do.

The men look for eagles. None.
After three hours the men mizzle off.

It is raining, and there are no birds.
It is a long slipping march back to the city.

Shiva starts counting enemies.
Christ's forehead begins to bleed,
Mecca turns men like a compass point,
Hands find hilts, heads are covered,
A stomach swells with warm and worshipful breath,
And all else is reversed and forgotten.

They should have waited nine.

The blade becomes a babe with reflective skin;
The embrace is never fruitless.

She climbs out of the dark sticky body.
On her flesh, Athena shows the clouds.

The daggers of her teeth curve with her thoughts;
The father outwitted – no, inwitted – by the daughter.

Out of any, he wore an old shape too long;
When the altars emptied his death came all the quicker.

James McLaughlin

Man in a Hole

there were no signs of violence
his body intact
no incursions were found into his territory
nothing in his hut had been disturbed
indigenous expert Marcos Dos Santos said
to local media outlets in Brazil
he was the sole survivor after
the rest of his tribe had been killed
by illegal miners in 1995
his name was not known and
he lived in total isolation for 26 years
he was known as the *man of the hole*
he dug deep holes some
of which he used to trap animals
others he used to hide in he
was *uncontacted* having never been
in touch with the outside world
and he avoided ALL contact
he had been monitored for many
decades by Funia and other agencies
his body was found emaciated
in a hammock outside his hut knowing
he was going to die he
covered himself in Macaw feathers
to many indigenous tribes the
Macaw is almost Godlike
it is seen by them as the symbol of the sun
that brings healing through
colour and light it is also the mark
of fertility to the rain forests as
they forage for fruits and nuts
then drop seeds through their excrement
that propagates life in undergrowth

it represents grace and ease
to the indigenous tribes it
is the guardian the protector of the air
of the winds carrying prayers
to the heavens it evokes a sense of magic
of song and communication it
can mimic the human voice
that same human voice now silent
in a hammock coffin that voice
that once filled the forests
and river banks that spoke
to the birds and angles
and carried invocations
where dinosaurs roamed
and pterodactyls flew

1969 Muffie

he had an overwhelming desire
to do it for her
he smiled trying to remember the two-year-old
she loved to slide down the sand pit
he permitted himself a moment
before the silver crater
Armstrong's face clouded over
when American journalist Ed Bradley
brought up the subject
I thought the best thing to do
was to carry on as normal try
as hard as I could to
keep going for the sake
of my family at the time
I thought my family was handling
it well and I was doing my best
the First Man mumbled
as he always mumbled then
he jumped in the air
and slide down the crater legs
in the air laughin like
a child swimming
upsidedown all alone in
a Sea of Tranquillity

Maurice Scully

Note

As a little boy on the farm he played every day with water, what he
called his stream, a small stretch of rainwater on a hill in a boreen
to the side of the house leading down to the lake & some meadows beyond.
Its little pools, falls, smells, light-flickerings, the sparkling patterns of flow,
his fingers busy with pebbles & grass & the cool fluid, combined a hypnotic
delight. Dark mud soft between toes. Narrative. When he returned to the city
for the winter his uncle sent a card, drawing 'yr stream' as a diagonal line thus:

Events & perceptions are elastic in time. Shocked, the 4-year-old boy
found it difficult to believe. His stream was much, much more, much
more even in outline, even thus:

This was the earliest realization that he remembers.

Chords

Women ululating in the village – some excitement, a young man
returning from the mines, safe, sober, a marriage arranged,
the bride-price agreed, negotiations complete…

> *the Potters the Cotters the Cutlers the Glovers*
> *the Sheppards the Sawyers the Falkners the Farmers*

A rock on a hill from the top of which can be seen the roof of his grandfather's
farmhouse (whom he never knew) nestled among sheltering cypress below;
to the west, a lake, sunset over distant mountains; to the south, a small meadow
on the side of a drumlin, oats, hay – green, gold – ready for harvest both…

> *the Baxters the Bakers the Millers the Mercers*
> *the Skinners the Pinners the Wellers the Wheelers*

Formal movements, almost-silent, pock. A box-bedroom overlooking
playing fields with white-clad cricketers practising their formal dance
with, & in, quiet. Beyond the fringe of the Phoenix Park, pale blue hills
in outline. He is working at his desk, reading, taking notes, a young man,
starting out, looking in. Thin ice.

> *a hut in a garden   a patch to weed   a seat under a tree*
> *the Coopers the Smiths the Pages the Singers*

Sound of a pen moving along a page, tip, scratch, flow, left to right, & down,
left to right, & on, twisted, puzzling in the rough, inch by inch, its lingo,
delete, re-write, re-think, continue…

> *the Websters the Clerks the Palmers the Fullers*
> *the Toners the Taylors the Turners*

Kneeling to weed a patch in the gravel in the high summer of his 70th
year, he rights some upturned woodlice, with held breath, with care,
a moment, that amble off then through the millennia under blue-grey
pebbles by the path…

the Walkers the Wallers the Woodmans the Masons
the Fishers the Fletchers the Chandlers the Chapmans

They sat on a seat under a sycamore over 50 years ago. Summer.
Suddenly she kissed him, without prelude, soft, threshold, a tremor
of excitement on the lips, apple-taste, abrupt & lovely, their large
brains, flexible intellects, new bodies…

puzzling in the rough   blue-grey pebbles by the path

summer under a flickering tree   the idea of peace   that

The Piano

My brother played the piano. My brother played the piano & practised
scales assiduously. My brother was taught & mentored by a blind composer.
Sometimes, as a child, I went along with my brother, ten years my senior,
to sit, fascinated, in his teacher's music room while they went over lessons
on the black glossy baby grand in the centre of the floor. There was a
large mirror over the marble fireplace with a rising line of ducks in flight
made I think of faded coloured felt glued to the glass as if leaving a river
or a lake. My brother was good. His tutor saw (heard/felt) promise. There
was a stucco rose in the centre of the ceiling & decorations at each corner.
Behind me there were two high windows reaching it seemed to the ceiling
far above. The windows had long yellow drapes reaching to the floor. This
was an old & old-fashioned house.

My brother played the usual repertoire. To a child, familiar… My brother
played forever, it seemed forever, wearing out the old family piano, until he
bought a new one, a good quality upright that he set to work on immediately
to make it pay its way. Scales, bits of concertos, this & that that took his
fancy at the time.

My brother's teacher married & moved away. My brother began to hear
voices. He began to see terrifying visions. He believed 'a syndicate' was in
pursuit, to kill him. My brother's mind split.

Then he stopped playing classical music altogether & had the piano re-tuned. He began playing rag-time. First, a range of rag-time composers, then one, then only one piece by that composer, then only the opening bars of that one piece, by that composer, over & over & over again, getting it *perfect*. He felt it was not perfect. He held to his belief that complete perfection was within his reach. He played & he played with great vehemence & concentration the opening bars. The opening bars were the key to the whole piece. His conviction led him on & on. He would unlock the flow of the whole piece if he nailed the opening bars. Nailed these completely. This was possible.

His talent narrowed. Sharpened. His talent began to overwhelm. The voices & visions increased. He left his job. It was no longer possible to function in that world. He practised all the more.

I began to write poetry around this time, very bad poetry, to be sure. I believed though, I could learn & come closer to unlocking the flow of the real thing, unhampered by visions & voices. My mind did not split. Dark-ness came, certainly, but it did not split. Practice, I practised. I still practise, I practise every day. Many years have passed. My brother is dead 20 years now. And I ... keeping focus. Here. Someday, who knows, the opening bars.

Peter Robinson

Bird Life

for my daughter

Giving way to a mother and child-in-arms
on one of those daily excursions,
I might be helping reclaim the streets
perhaps, but not the night,
Giulia, now your planned
vigil on Clapham Common has been banned
under their pandemic regulations...
I'm on the park in daylight and a world of harms.

Those Egyptian geese with their single chick
are honking at a large brown rat.
Another pair with brood of four
have lost one I counted days before,
worried how many of their five
would in the end survive.

And nor can I help fearing for relations
still not home now darkness falls
when over this ruffled lake's surface
one clattering, great-winged swan takes off
like something imagined by a Howard Hughes...

After all these years, I'm no less haunted
by those whose power's put on with their violence
(when attentions are unwanted)
and like two lines of Zadkine sculptures
an avenue's pollarded limbs are
pleading to the skies if that makes sense.

Rumoured

'an ambassador is an honest gentleman
sent to lie abroad for his country'
　　　　—Sir Henry Wootton

1

Under magniloquent murals
with victors' magnanimous gestures,
the gifts from distant subject peoples,
you show us shabby showcases
while the Minister in a tight huddle
with her advisors is going places…

2

Past an ambassadors' waiting room
where honest gentlemen readied their lies
(using abroad ones practised at home),
along the carpeted corridors stacked
with white-goods cardboard boxes,
your workplace, it's a museum.

3

From a blank PowerPoint screen
intruded on the draped, high ceiling,
red-plush conference rooms
and martial or field-marshal portraits
in the India, the Locarno, comes
a sense of false dimensions.

4

They each have chronic statue problems:
Sir Anthony Eden, for instance,
his bronze bust at a stairhead

with dark-wood banister rail
polished by all those diplomatic hands
that did or didn't sign the paper.

5

Nations' flags droop in dim daylight
glimpsed around the Cenotaph
through windows where their guests would sit,
Lord Grey's words come haunting back
about lamps going out, or Pitt
on rolling up the map of Europe...

6

Most of all, a rumoured serpent
promised by those Empire Windrush,
wryly allusive entrance guards
(their welcome, jesting words
would set me at my ease),
it's only a stuffed one in the Library.

7

We wouldn't find it on our tour,
but once outside, the gardens'
stretched silhouettes of trees,
what could they be pointing towards
when down each muted corridor
even the statues look eager for peace?

August 2022

Emily Tristan Jones

A Concession

A crow and her accessory entertain the idea
of my yard for a minute

I note them on my petty day

She walks like an Egyptian on the ridge of the shed. And descends
to the vegetable
beds

Fixates on a hinge in a folding chair

and then orients again to their route in the air

Is she unimpressed by my layout?
From my door I would like to tell her:
They might call what I do to languish,
but I am at peace with this

And if she spoke English:

Emily, don't worry yourself
I can make sense of all equivalents

There is not the mystery you make it out to be

in my non-woman heart

V

I want to be able to open a book and read it with one hand
But there's the jacket to deal with and the wind

And when I get around to it, I am distracted by my womanly
hands

I have divined with them
I've slandered, I've slated meetings on your soul

I've also pressed gently into rooms, my own soul to follow
I've made occasions to be comfortable
and those to nearly fall from and die

I've thrown my hands onto scissors, forming the flash of a V in the air
and they've automatically cut flowers to lengths
for a preserves jar

But to hold a book is rough
as the stars are dim and my eyes are rolling

G.C. Waldrep

Elegy for Everything in the Path of HS2

infinity's stroke
laid to the field's
stiff monstrance
its indivisible
word pronounced

once, twice
not by silence
but as a veil towards
which silence
inclines, & adjusts

—*exchange gods*
I thought I read
(in that grammar's
flat imperative)
(but the eye's day
is the soul's night)

in the niche
of apostolic craft
each museum
crucifies its one
brass key

indignant glass
of weak
division, bind
my vagrant wound

bell or wolf
the master testifies
(turning from
his televised trial)

Icklingham All Saints

a blur some tooth
hallucinated

the wind chalks it
up, & then
back down again

the wave offering,
the heave offering,
blind flutes

the wind traces
on wax paper

(but does not play)

my lesioned feet
no longer spoke
the glory-tongue

in the spare room
containing
two veiled plinths

the solstice,
towards which
the voice inclines

sheaths
for the peonies'
Fauvist tractions

there,
in the stretch
of intact shadows

Synoptic Gospel

The immersive flow.
recoilless
amid the Januaries
of memory—

A wren lights upon it.

New nation, new
subject-assemblage.

The depths
staked
as against light,
though not unkindly.

I lock
myself out, an edge.

No *harvest*, no
return.
Gravity-fed
among the witnesses.

Your eye
deep in the eye-dark
activating.
The *-ness* of this.

Wren-shaped
absence occulting.

Witness Psalm
flame azaleas, Sugar Grove, North Carolina

perplex of unmitigated
      exteriority

absence
presses into, a limit—

      the necessary

a grammar
oblique in first-light

circumambulant *thou*

(it knows the law,
      or it is a law)

affirmed
in the court
of precedence, a sign

      which is exile

the event, ascendant

the intermediate gaze

Nóra Blascsók

Liver paté

innards wobble like that bit of liver grandmother served
on a summer evening spread on a slice with fat I remember
now the liver wasn't wobbly it was hard to spread chunks of it

on my tongue heavy like dead animal me not uneasy yet about
eating dead flesh - one day I'll be in the middle of the road
same turn every day driving and the deer that appears

from the trees is me 30 years ago wait 40 years ago wide-eyed
not expecting bad things the worst that could happen is
a paw tangled up in ivy or I could be hit by a car guess

that's something that can always happen if you're 5 or a deer
you don't expect your life could end any moment bam
and I will be remembered by fellow deer or it will be my absence

they notice but carry on as if nothing happened as I lie on the road
driver above scratching her head or throwing up depending on degree
of discomfort around fresh blood or innards not knowing what to do

first clean up dial some helpline need to get the order right
open the glove box let the serrated edge do the work move it
back and forward

Get me there

moving through / landscape of lampposts / bare
trees / tram driving into screensaver stills / tracks
disappear under / neath look straight a head /
driver's bald patch / for your own safety / don't set /
fire to things / advice I like / to live / by have you
paid / for this journey oh yes / I have every morning
/ jelly across the street / skin friction against fabric /
breathe enough air to / last three zones / step in

Kenny Knight

The Ghost Writers Club

Words linger on your lips
like the sweetness
of a Suzanne Vega song
every time you read to yourself
every ghost writer in the room listens.

A first draft of free verse
drops into the accumulated dust
of years on your writing table
your pen has done a bunk
into the domestic clutter
so you write and you write
your latest masterpiece
with a stick of chalk
like a primary school teacher.

The sun slips under the door
of your writing room
makes the house shine
your eyes follow it
until it slips into the west.

Darkness falls
like a power cut.
Sleep is a stranger
who comes in the night
doesn't tell you it's name.

The darkness isn't afraid of itself
the darkness is afraid of the light
but has learned to push
the scary blueness away.

Unseen by you a ghost writer
looks nostalgically over your shoulder
as it takes a short cut
through the architecture
of the Ghost Town Street
Ghost Writers Club.

You take a break
from making language
out of a city
out of a white space
you take a flashback
of a nineteen sixty seven
transatlantic telephone call
into the kitchen
which is interrupted
by a very noisy washing machine
reading ink stains to itself.

You think about leaving here
knowing it's not easy to leave
the road you've travelled
to go guitar solo all by yourself
to hear that lonesome sound
and not sigh
when a steam train leaves town
in a grumble of smoke.

Anna Akhmatova

translated by Stephen Capus

The King with Grey Eyes

Hail, infinite grief! The king with grey eyes
Is dead, but my sorrow will never subside.

Autumn glowed red as the evening grew dark;
My husband came home and calmly remarked:

'He'd gone out to hunt by himself all day;
He was found beneath the old oak tree, they say.

I pity the queen: in the space of one night,
Although she's still young, her hair has turned white!'

From above the fire-place he took down his pipe
And went off to the work which detains him each night.

And now I must wake my child right away
And gaze at her beautiful eyes of grey;

While through the window the poplars sing:
'The earth is no longer home to your king...'

11 September 1910
Tsarskoe Selo

Lot's Wife

But behind him Lot's wife turned to look and became a pillar of salt.
— *The Book of Genesis*

And the one righteous man followed God's messenger,
Radiant and tall, up the lowering hill;
But her heart was disturbed by a nagging temptation:
Is it too late—or could she not still

Behold the lofty red towers of Sodom,
Her city, the yard where she worked, the square
Where she sang, and the house with its empty windows
Which she and her husband and children once shared.

So she turned to look—but her eyes could no longer
See through the pain by which they were bound;
And her body became a transparent column
Of salt, and her limbs were fixed to the ground.

Why should we weep for Lot's wife—she was surely
The least of the losses suffered that day?
Yet my heart can't forget that, for one last glance,
She was ready to throw her whole life away.

24 February 1924

Sketches from Komarovo

Oh, Muse of tears.
—Marina Tsvetaeva

I've withdrawn from all prospect of happiness here,
I've renounced all earthly goods;
The spirit which guards this place inhabits
A fallen tree in the wood.

Life is no more than a habit—like guests
We've come for just a few days;
And I seem to hear two voices conversing
Up there in the aerial ways.

Only two? In a thicket of raspberry bushes
By the eastern wall I can see
A dark green branch of elder. A letter,
Perhaps, from Marina to me?

19–20 November 1961

Mercè Rodoreda

translated by Rebecca Simpson

Three Sonnets from *World of Ulysses*

[Cyclops]¹

He twisted in this eye, oh my defenceless sheep,
the olive stake tempered in a pinewood fire.
The isle that you have trodden, royal mastiff,
has given you –sweeter than your wine– my blood!

You too will suffer, Nobody, all pain awaits you,
the blue wind of the bay-tree scorching heaven's sphere,
my hands are blind and cannot undo
this knot of thought, little whelp of a wild beast.

Gaze emptied of green and of high pink dusks,
a vegetable calm settles on my tongue,
colours silent, the overwhelming howl ...

Avenge me, oh high jutting rocks; and you, patient cavern,
petition the gods to hammer into the depths of his past
longed for islands to make his land strange.

§

¹ Titles given by the editor of *Agonia de Llum – La poesia secreta
de Mercè Rodoreda* are in square brackets.

Why the sun should not rise yet

You will find it too much, like lead, your noon.
Dawn rouses the silver waves
about the land that fattened your livestock.
Oh sun! Halt your joyous leap:

for the one who –slipped into the great man's home–
doesn't know how to leave with the longed-for load;
for the two lovers whom a sigh has just parted;
for Polyphemus extending his long arms!

For the lowly fish burrowing in mud under stones;
for the mole that seeks darkness below;
for the ocelot silent in thorn-bed!

For the one still unborn who clings to the womb;
for those who don't move, stretched in earth's tomb;
for those who are living and that's where they'll head!

§

[Second evocation of the dead]

Under a pure sky reddened by the dawn
all struggling, my poor bats
kicked frantic aloft
on the cliff face of the bald rock.

I still see their pale faces
and the last wave of their exhausted hands;
voiceless then they called my name
each one from the depths of a wet throat.

Six heads washed back into the cave,
until a sudden blast of sea
swept the mysterious blue sands clear.

Over the choppy salt the rowers glided;
and in the terrified lakes of the gaze
the certain shadow of the dead resided.

§

Notes on Contributors

ANNA AKHMATOVA was born in Odesa in 1889 but lived most of her life in Saint Petersburg. Her first collection of poems, *Evening*, was published in 1912 and by the outbreak of World War 1 she was recognised as one of the leading contemporary Russian poets. Following the October Revolution she took the decision to remain in Russia and in her subsequent poetry she bore witness to the turbulent history of her country. She died in Moscow in 1966.

MARTIN ANDERSON has appeared in *Shearsman* many times, going all the way back to its beginnings over 40 years ago. His most recent collection is *A Country Without Names* (Shearsman Books, 2022).

NÓRA BLASCSÓK is a Hungarian poet based in Manchester. Her most recent poems can be found in *The Rialto, Butcher's Dog, bath magg* and *Acumen*. Her debut pamphlet titled *<body> of work </body>* was published by Broken Sleep Books in June 2022.

MELISSA BUCKHEIT is a queer poet, translator, activist, dancer and choreographer, photographer, English Lecturer and Orthopedic Massage Therapist, who lives in rural Northeast Connecticut. Her collection, *Noctilucent*, was published by Shearsman Books in 2012. Dancing Girl Press issued her chapbook, *Dulcet You* in 2016. She also translates the poetry of Ioulita Iliopoulou from Modern Greek.

STEPHEN CAPUS studied Russian language and literature at the University of Birmingham and the School of Slavonic and East European Studies, University of London. His translations have appeared in the *Penguin Book of Russian Poetry* (Penguin, 2015) and *Centres of Cataclysm* (Bloodaxe, 2016). His pamphlet *24 Hours* was published by Rack Press in 2020.

STUART COOKE's latest books are *Land Art* (Calanthe, 2022) and *Lyre* (UWAP, 2019). He is co-editor of *Transcultural Ecocriticism* (Bloomsbury, 2021). In 2023 he will be the BR Whiting Fellow in Rome, Italy. He lives in Brisbane, Australia, where he lectures in creative writing and literary studies at Griffith University.

CARRIE ETTER's most recent collection is *The Weather in Normal* (UK: Seren; US: Station Hill, 2018), a Poetry Book Society Recommendation.

AMY EVANS BAUER is an Anglo-Austrian poet based in London. Her five-chapbook poetic sequence includes *and umbels* (Jonathan Williams Chapbooks prize, Shirt Pocket Press, 2020) and three Shearsman titles. She performed its final sections, *SOUND((ING))S*, at the Institute of Contemporary Arts, London and internationally. Her poetry features in Queenzenglish.mp3 (Roof Books, 2020), *Chicago Review* and elsewhere. She is co-editor of *The Unruly Garden: Robert Duncan and Eric Mottram, Essays and Letters* (Peter Lang, 2007). She has written criticism for the British Library's Sound and Vision blog, and for BBC Radio 4.

ALEC FINLAY has two books from Shearsman, one a joint-venture with Ken Cockburn, and is also a practising artist. He lives in Edinburgh.

AMLANJYOTI GOSWAMI's most recent book of poetry, *Vital Signs* (Poetrywala) follows his widely reviewed collection, *River Wedding* (Poetrywala). He has reviewed poetry for *Modern Poetry in Translation* and has read in various places, including New York, Boston and Delhi. He grew up in Guwahati, Assam, and lives in Delhi.

DANIEL HINDS lives in Newcastle upon Tyne. He won the Poetry Society's Timothy Corsellis Young Critics Prize 2018. His poetry has been widely published in journals and anthologies and has been awarded several prizes.

EMILY TRISTAN JONES grew up in the subarctic and prairies. Her poems have been in *The Puritan, Harvard Review, Denver Quarterly, Dalhousie Review*, and several other journals. Her first book of poetry, *Buttercup*, will be published by Verge Books of Chicago in 2024. She holds a graduate degree in the visual arts from the University of Chicago. She lives in Montreal where she teaches poetry and edits *Columba*.

NORMAN JOPE lives in Plymouth and has authored several books, the most recent being *The Rest of the World* (Shearsman Books, 2021) .

KENNY KNIGHT is also from Plymouth, where he works in a supermarket, and runs CrossCountry Writers, and is co-editor of *Clutter* magazine. His most recent collection, *Love Poem to an Imaginary Girlfriend* was published by Shearsman Books in 2022.

MARY LEADER's most recent collection is *The Distaff Side* (2022), her third collection from Shearsman Books, and her fifth in all. She lives in Oklahoma.

ROB MACKENZIE lives in Leith, Scotland. His poetry collections are *The Opposite of Cabbage* (2009), *The Good News* (2013) and *The Book of Revelation* (2020), all published by Salt. A fourth collection, *Woof! Woof! Woof!* is due from Salt in Autumn 2023. He runs the literary publishing house, Blue Diode Press.

JAMES MCLAUGHLIN is an artist/poet who lives in Dumbarton, Scotland. He has published two collections with Knives Forks and Spoons Press, among others.

At the time of her death, aged 22, in 2014, **SOPHIA NUGENT-SIEGAL** was a post-graduate student in ancient history at Macquarie University, Melbourne, from which she also held a undergraduate degree in ancient history. She was a poet and an emerging author of speculative-fiction. Periods of her youth had been spent in Italy and England, which influenced her work and study. Her poetry collection, *Oracle*, was published in 2007, when she was 16. The poem printed here is previously unpublished.

ELIZA O'TOOLE has a PhD from the University of Essex where she walked among experimental poets of note. Her first collection of poetry, *The Dropping of Petals,* was published in 2021 by Muscaliet Press. Muscaliet is publishing her second collection, *The Formation of Abscission Layers,* this year.

MICHELLE PENN is the author of a book-length poem, *Paper Crusade* (Arachne Press, 2022), and a pamphlet, *Self-portrait as a diviner, failing* (Paper Swans Press, 2018). Recent poetry has appeared in *The London Magazine, Bad Lilies and PN Review*. Michelle plans innovative events in London as part of Corrupted Poetry.

PETER ROBINSON's most recent collection of poetry is *Retrieved Attachments,* published by Two Rivers Press to celebrate his seventieth birthday. His *Collected Poems*

1976–2016, The Personal Art: Essays, Memoirs & Reviews, and *Peter Robinson: A Portrait of his Work*, ed. Tom Phillips are available from Shearsman Books.

JAIME ROBLES is a writer and book artist. Her poetry collections *Anime Animus Anima* and *Hoard* were published by Shearsman Books. Her most recent book was *Soundtracks* (Woodland Editions, 2019). She lives in the San Francisco Bay Area and is currently working on a collection of poems about fire.

MERCÈ RODOREDA (1908–1983) began writing poetry while in exile in France. She always wrote in her native Catalan and her chosen form was the sonnet. Notwithstanding the quality of the works, and prizes won, few were published before Rodoreda resolved to dedicate herself exclusively to fiction. She is considered by many to be the greatest Catalan novelist of the 20th century. In 2002, 105 sonnets were collected in the book *Agonia de Llum – la poesia secreta de Mercè Rodoreda*, which was republished in 2022.

MAURICE SCULLY published many books, most recently *Play Book* (Coracle Press, 2019), *Things That Happen* (Shearsman, 2020) and *Airs* (Shearsman, 2022). A book of essays on his work, *A Line of Tiny Zeros in the Fabric*, edited by Ken Keating, also appeared from Shearsman in 2020. Sadly, Maurice passed away in March 2023.

AIDAN SEMMENS moved last year from Suffolk to Orkney. His sixth book, *The Jazz Age*, was published last October by Salt; four previous volumes came from Shearsman.

NATHAN SHEPHERDSON lives in Queensland; his most recent publication is *how to spear sleep* (Shearsman Books, 2021).

REBECCA SIMPSON is a translator based in Barcelona. She has translated both poetry and opera libretti, and an anthology of her translations of Joan Brossa, Rafael Alberti, León Felipe and Joan Miró will soon by published by the A34 Gallery in Barcelona.

M. STASIAK grew up in Newfoundland and now lives and works in London. Her work has been published in magazines including *Magma, The Rialto, Brittle Star, Envoi, Iota, Interpreter's House, Urthona, The North, Poetry Salzburg Review, Shearsman* and *Long Poem Magazine*. Her chapbook *Enchant/extinguish* was published in August 2021 by Shearsman Books.

COLE SWENSEN has written 19 books of poetry, most recently *Art in Time* (Nightboat, 2021). A former Guggenheim Fellow, recipient of the Iowa Poetry Prize and the PEN USA Award in Translation, among others, and a finalist for the National Book Award, she lives in France and the US, where she teaches at Brown University.

G.C. WALDREP is a poet and historian who teaches at Bucknell University, Pennsylvania. His most recent book is *The Earliest Witnesses* (Carcanet Press and Tupelo Press, USA, 2021).

CARL WALSH lives and writes in Australia on Wurundjeri land. His work has been published in journals such as *StylusLit, Rabbit, Meanjin, Westerly, Wales Haiku Journal* and *Poetry for the Planet: An Anthology of Imagined Futures*. His first book of poetry is slated for publication in 2023/24 as part of the Flying Islands Pocket Poets series.

PETRA WHITE is an Australian poet living in Berlin. Her most recent collection is *Cities* (Vagabond Press 2021).